Made with love
for all children of the world.

Dedicated to my
rainbow baby,
Swayze Yegen.

Special thanks to my husband, Kris, for encouraging me every day and believing in me and in this book. I couldn't have done it without you.

Visit www.rachaelrosezoller.com for a free downloadable childrens chakra coloring page!

Text and illustrations © Rachael Rose Zoller 2016
Printed by createspace
Available from Amazon.com & other retail outlets
First Edition.

MY BODY IS A RAINBOW

A BOOK ABOUT OUR CHAKRAS

WRITTEN & ILLUSTRATED BY

RACHAEL ROSE ZOLLER

My body is a rainbow.
I am filled with colors,
light and love!

I have seven swirling
chakras, they are each
unique because...

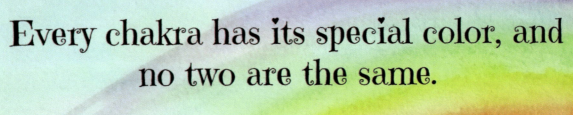

Every chakra has its special color, and no two are the same.

All of my chakras make a
RAINBOW!

red
orange
yellow

green

blue

indigo

and violet too.

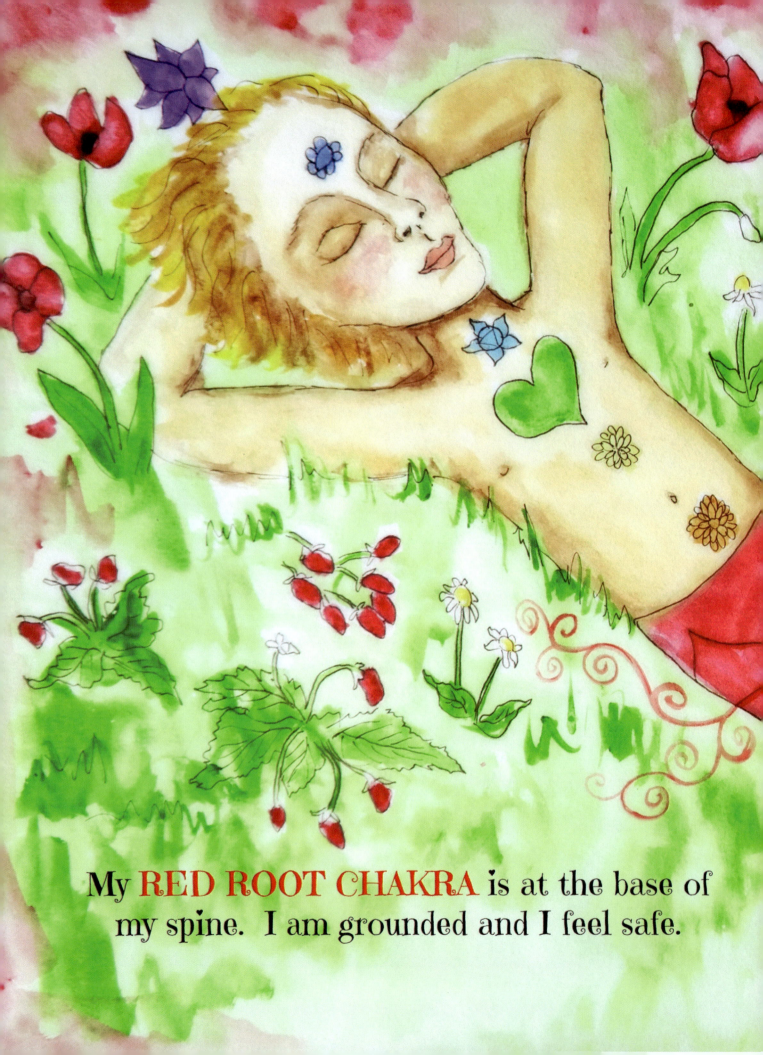

My RED ROOT CHAKRA is at the base of my spine. I am grounded and I feel safe.

I send energy to my root chakra when my bare feet touch the earth.

My **ORANGE SACRAL CHAKRA** is below my belly button.

I am grateful and at ease.

I freely share my gifts with others and recieve abundance in return.

My **YELLOW SOLAR PLEXUS CHAKRA** is above my belly button.

I am full of energy and strength.

When I feel happy and strong, my goals and dreams come true!

My GREEN HEART CHAKRA is filled
with compassion and love.

Place your hand on your heart and say;
I give love, I feel love, I am love.

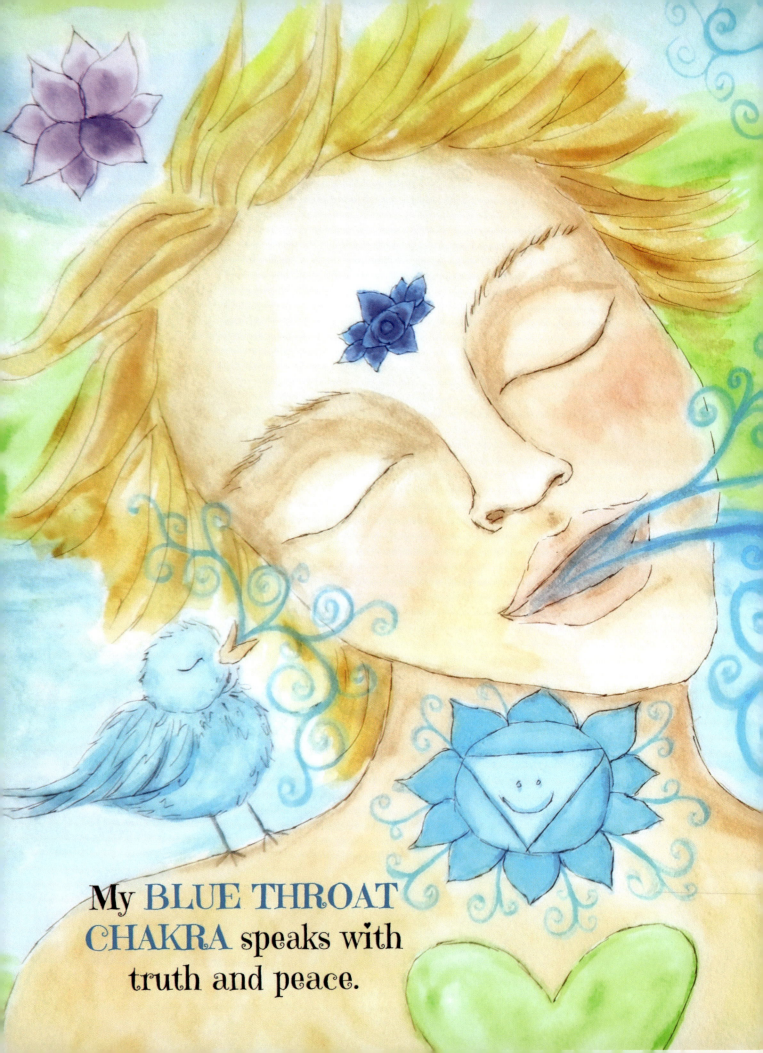

My BLUE THROAT
CHAKRA speaks with
truth and peace.

I am creative and
I love to express
myself with my
voice, my art, and
while I play.

My **INDIGO THIRD EYE CHAKRA** is
an invisible inner eye.
My third eye is intuitive and helps me to
sense things that my other two eyes
cannot see...

Like
thoughts,
feelings,
ideas,
dreams
and energy.

My
VIOLET CROWN CHAKRA
is a beautiful lotus
that sits upon my head.
This lotus is always
growing and blooming,
just like me and you.

Our crown chakra
connects us
to all humans,
plants,
and creatures
of the world.

I have inner wisdom
that helps me
make good choices.
I love myself and
I feel love around me
at all times.

I am in harmony
with the entire
universe
and so are you.

Now we have reached the end
of this rainbow chakra book.

May you always remember
that you are a
sacred and beautiful rainbow.

You are here to love
and to share your special gifts.

Do you know what happens
when you share and spread love?

You make
the entire world
HAPPY!

Namaste

35777546R00018

Printed in Great Britain
by Amazon